CLB 1518
Photography by David Levenson/Colorific!
©1985 Illustrations and text: Colour Library Books Ltd.,
    Guildford, Surrey, England.
All rights reserved.
1985 edition published by Crescent Books, distributed
    by Crown Publishers, Inc.
Printed in Spain.
ISBN 0 517 60568 6
h g f e d c b a

CHARLES and DIANA
IN AMERICA

CRESCENT BOOKS
NEW YORK

It wasn't, praise be, a State visit. State visits are formal, predictable affairs, regimented and protocol-ridden. Despite months of meticulous planning and hellish security, this first visit by Prince Charles and Princess Diana to the land their forebears ceded was alive with informality, surprise, youthfulness, levity and poignancy. It had its official justification, of course, but that didn't spoil a thing.

You can't, after all, afford to be pompous about these things in the States. Only there could a restauranteur offer the royal couple a free meal and be interviewed at length on television when turned down. Only there would a Californian artist trudge to Washington to show off his Diana mural, fashioned from 10,000 jelly-beans. Only there would they try to balance a Rolls-Royce on four Wedgwood coffee cups. Only there would anyone have the nerve to fly a banner across the sky above Prince Charles' polo match, inviting: "Tennis tomorrow, Diana?"

It was from the start a cathartic experience for those nursing a five-year-old ambition to meet Diana: for young Ann Waymire, who didn't get her autograph, but was shown her engagement ring, and who then burst into tears; for the Smith twins and their friend from Reading, Pennsylvania, who spent a night on Washington Cathedral steps because "she's glamorous and he's going to be the next King of England"; for Jonathan Lollar, suffering from an inoperable brain tumour, who deemed it, realistically, "one of my last thrills" to speak with the Princess; and for 67-year-old Edith Pittman, terminally ill with lung cancer, whom Diana greeted by name. "I've never been treated like this before," she said afterwards. "Maybe my living has not been in vain."

For the mere spectators, the media had orchestrated things grandly. No magazine worthy of the name missed the chance to sport the couple on its front cover, and where there was a choice, Diana was it. One newspaper carried a full page of questions about her, answered unofficially for her by James Whitaker of the *Daily Mirror* who knows she shaves her legs and boasts of having touched her bottom in New Zealand. Even the staid *Washington Post* advised those likely to be introduced what *not* to ask in the royal presence. And the ABC network paid £$\frac{1}{2}$ million to screen ITV's interview with the Prince and Princess on the eve of their arrival.

The events of the tour, well documented in pictures here, were many and the couple worked hard and fast. Inevitably a few events took the mind off the rest and made it a tour of sheer splendour. Opulent dinners, a spectacular gala, dazzling shop displays and a magnificent exhibition drew ever larger gasps. The list of famous names seemed endless: not just the Reagans, Bushes and Shultzes, but Gloria Vanderbilt, David Hockney, Bob Hope, Victor Borge, Peter Ustinov, Eva Gabor, Norman Parkinson and Cary Grant. Leontyne Price sang at the White House dinner, while Diana danced with Clint Eastwood, Neil Diamond and John Travolta ("I'll give her ten out of ten"). In Palm Beach she danced with Gregory Peck, and Prince Charles took the floor with Joan Collins.

There were, of course, minor disasters. The IRA barracked and flew banners. President Reagan called Diana "David", and a jet-lagged Prince Charles forgot to toast his host. The occasional Union Jack was spotted upside-down. Joan Collins nearly upstaged the Princess by arriving, dripping with jewels, just when Diana was due. Prince Charles nearly lost his swimming trunks while surfing in Hawaii. Some of the Best of Britain merchandise was made in Korea. There were pockets of apathy, antipathy and jealousy.

But few people, either in Britain or America, will look back with bitterness, or even indifference. The trip was, by any standards, a catalogue of superlatives which the host nation was not slow to express. "Americans are given to crazes, and the Prince and Princess have become the latest," said one. Another described the excitement they generated as exceeding "anything since the British burned our capital". The wealthy socialites who secured invitations to dinners ransacked their family vaults to produce outsize jewellery for the occasion, or went to Emanuels for their gowns. The weather was perfection, the sunshine brilliant, the royal progress triumphal, and the television time generous. Diana's clothes, mostly new and restricted almost entirely to reds, whites and blues - were more than a match for the sparkle that greeted her.

In short, Washington and Palm Beach were willing, wooed and won, and the rest of America watched the proceedings with envy. For five days the Statue of Liberty wore a sweeping hairstyle, an heirloom tiara and a modest smile. And her people smiled with her.

The arrival predicted the
shape of things to come.
Washington officials
(above) beamed; tiny
children hugged their
royal heroine (left) or gave
her flowers (right); while
Diana requited the last
wish of young Jonathan
Lollar, terminally ill with
a brain tumour, by
accepting his record album
of gospel music (top left).

Indicative of the tight security characterising the entire visit, a helicopter (above) whisked the Prince and Princess to the White House (left) to be welcomed by Mr and Mrs Reagan (top). Despite the President's suave appearance in a plaid jacket that proclaimed his part-Scottish ancestry, and some jokey conversation (previous pages) between the world's four most famous personalities, the presidential couple seemed a little overawed by their young guests. After a photo-call (overleaf) the hosts nervously nudged and wrong-footed each other and the royal couple (opposite) into the cool elegance of their official home.

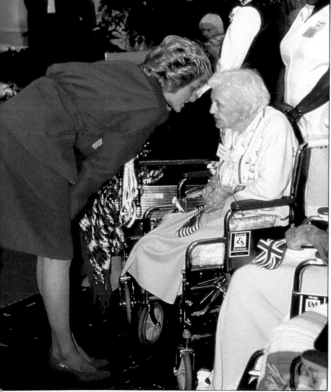

A red carpet welcome for Princess Diana brought her to the Washington Home, where those with incurable diseases can live with dignity. A word in the royal ear (above) and the fragrance of a princess' bouquet (top) made life truly worth living.

The Reagans emerged from the White House (above) to greet the Windsors that evening for dinner. Prince Charles was his usual urbane self as (top) he met the President, but it was his wife who made a stunning impact in her midnight blue velvet ball gown (left). Perhaps she and Nancy had arranged things to produce the brilliant "ligh and dark" effect of their contrasting dresses (opposite) as they posed with their husbands (following pages) before dinner. The menu (said t have reflected royal tastes included lobster, crab an glazed chicken, followed by peach sorbet, Californian wines and Champagne.

NATIONAL GALLERY
OF ART
WASHINGTON,

Diana (opposite) smiled
through her husband's
speech at the *Treasure
Houses of Britain*
exhibition. Her large,
face-concealing hat (top

left) and contrasting lapels
(left) were pure chic,
though they didn't stop
Charles cracking yet
another joke at her
expense (above).

NATIONAL GALL
OF ART
WASHINGTON, I

Dinner at the British Embassy meant a long dress and tiara, and once again Diana did not fail to meet the challenge. A daintily scalloped lace evening gown with taffeta skirt and see-through lace sleeves was as dazzling as that famous Queen Mary tiara. As the President rarely attends embassy socials, Vice-President and Mrs Bush were the guests of honour (overleaf).

It seemed appropriate that the husband and wife team regarded by the world as personifying the best of Britain should patronise a retail trade drive bearing that very title. The firm of J.C. Penney, trying - successfully it seems - to spruce up its image, was host, and the huge crowd's home-made placards said it all as Charles and Diana arrived (right and opposite) at the Springfield store to tour some fabulous displays which could only remind them of home.

Replica Crown jewels and period costumes (opposite page, below left), and the glittering gold and silver of Penney's massive displays (top and opposite page, top) contrasted with the drab security round

the Prince and Princess.
The visitors inspected the
clothes department, Prince
Charles chatting to staff
(top); his wife reminding
her host that the Prince's

double-breasted jackets
ought to be followed by
Americans. At least the
Press (above) had a good
view of the Prince's style.

After a visit with Mrs Reagan to Springfield's Drug Rehabilitation Center (previous four pages), Diana joined her husband for a Remembrance ceremony at Arlington cemetery: solemnity amid perfect fall weather, the gold and rust backdrop of leaves and the vivid patterns of flags.

As his mother, the Queen, had done in London the previous day, so Prince Charles led the homage at Arlington, laying a huge wreath (right) of cream chrysanthemums and dahlias splashed with a burst of red blooms, at a memorial to the unknown dead of two world wars.

The final engagement of a hectic three-day stay in Washington took the Prince and Princess back to the National Gallery of Art for a dinner to acknowledge their patronage of the *Treasure* *Houses of Britain* exhibition. For once, Diana resurrected a well-known evening dress, with its daring, off-the-shoulder look, its spangled fabric and its slim cut.

Everything seemed more relaxed at Palm Beach where, after only three hours' sleep, Charles and Diana arrived next day. With sideline royalty (top right) and Disneyland royalty (above) in predictable dress, Britain's royal lady chose a loose, jaunty outfit (right). A single flower (opposite) replaced the formal bouquet, and she was, at last, surrounded only by personal friends (top).

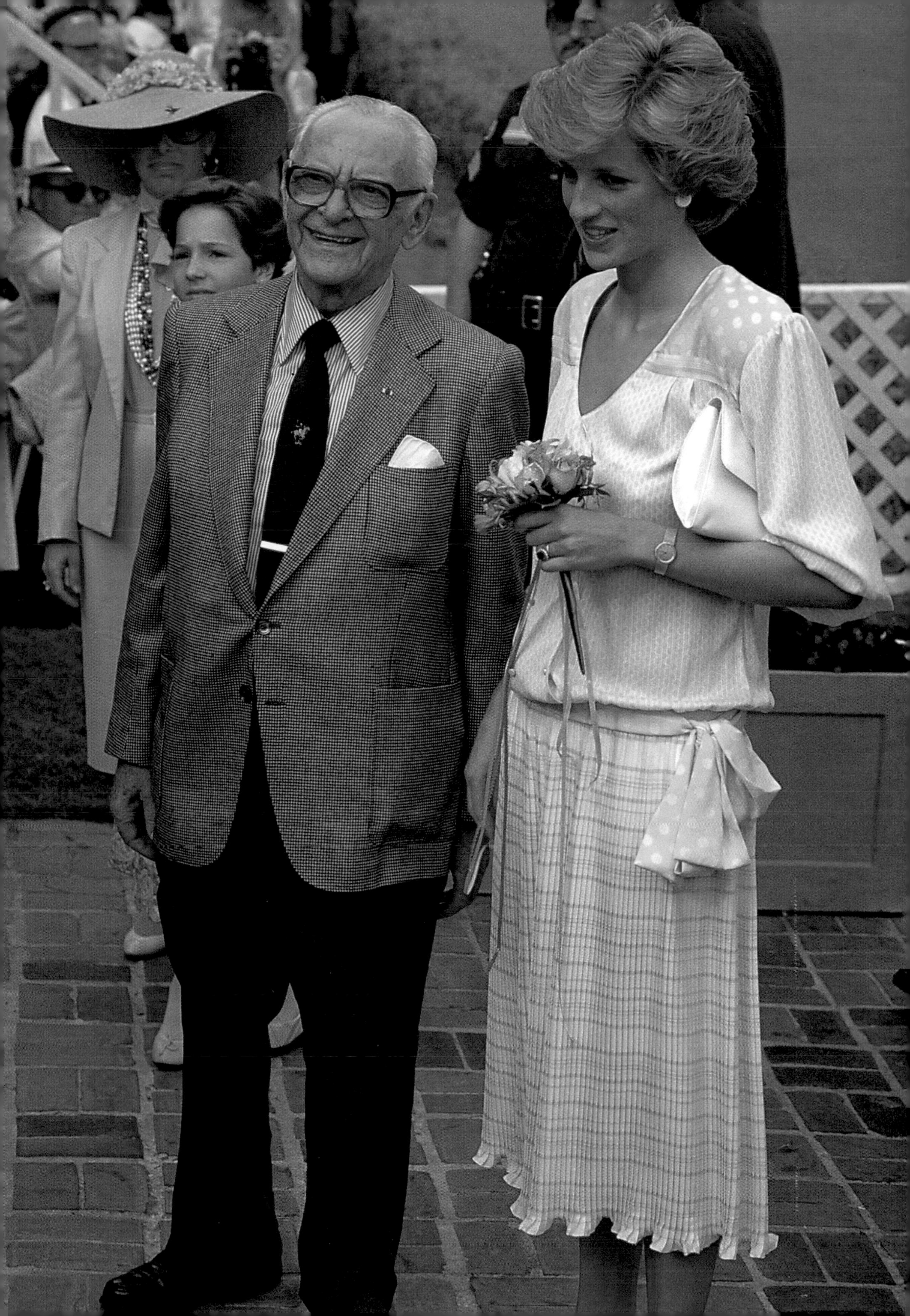

The weather, which had been at its best in Washington, was perfect in Florida, and in 80°F Prince Charles played some of his best polo. Though out of practice since August, he made some fast moves and, as if by arrangement, scored the winning goal to frenetic shrieking and cheering from a large female contingent. Last time he played polo in Florida, he collapsed with heat exhaustion!

The game *wasn't* rigged, of course. "You don't let the Prince's team win just because he's a prince," said one of his regular team-mates. "You have to bump him as hard as he bumps you, otherwise he creams you." But one benefit of being a polo-playing Prince is that a member of the family is often there to present the prizes. So Diana came forward to do the honour (left and opposite page, top) and have a quick word with the victors (above and top) who subsequently held aloft

their magnificent trophy (previous page, bottom). In addition, the Prince received another of those very public kisses from his wife, who seems to enjoy polo every bit as much as she says she does. Memories of those infamous early days when Press and people went to polo matches merely to hound her have surely faded. These pictures of her relaxing with friends (top) and waving a cheery farewell as she and Prince Charles climbed back into their car (opposite page) show how far the image of her antipathy to her husband's favourite sport has changed in four years.

Climaxing the tour, the dinner-dance at Palm Beach's Breakers Hotel was a gala *par excellence*. Wealth, glamour and royalty combined to make it the social event of the season. Ladies turned up in their opulent best (above), along with stars like Bob Hope (right) and Joan Collins, with new husband Peter Holm (above left; opposite right). Despite Charles' apparent reservations (left), Diana's rich, raspberry velvet dress was a winner.

The gala raised $4 million for the United World Colleges, so the visitors left for home in good humour next morning. Snatched conversations, dropped curtseys, affable handshakes and (opposite) a wave of thanks and good wishes filled the last moments of their superbly successful tour.